Leading from the Lockers:
Guided Journal

John C. Maxwell
Leadership Books for Students

(Based on *Developing the Leader Within You*)

Leading from the Lockers:
Student Edition
ISBN 0-8499-7722-3

Leading from the Lockers:
Guided Journal
ISBN 0-8499-7723-1

The PowerPak Series

Leading Your Sports Team
ISBN 0-8499-7725-8

Leading in Your Youth Group
ISBN 0-8499-7726-6

Leading at School
ISBN 0-8499-7724-X

Leading As a Friend
ISBN 0-8499-7727-4

"These books are outstanding. John Maxwell's leadership principles have been communicated in a way that any student can understand and practice. Take them and go make a difference in your world."

—Dr. Tim Elmore,
Vice President of Leadership Development, EQUIP;
Author of *Nurturing the Leader in Your Child*

Leading from the Lockers:
Guided Journal

by
John C. Maxwell
with
Tama Fortner

Thomas Nelson, Inc. • Nashville

LEADING FROM THE LOCKERS: GUIDED JOURNAL

Based on John C. Maxwell's *Developing the Leader Within You.*

Copyright © 2001 by Injoy Inc.

Cartoon art copyright © Bobby Gombert 2001.

Published in Nashville, Tennessee, by Tommy Nelson®, a division of Thomas Nelson, Inc.

Special thanks to Ron Luce and Teen Mania for providing research materials for this book.

Unless otherwise indicated, Scripture quotations are from the *International Children's Bible, New Century Version*, copyright © 1983, 1986, 1988.

Scripture quotations marked (NKJV) are from the NEW KING JAMES VERSION of the Bible. Copyright © 1979, 1980, 1982, Thomas Nelson, Inc., Publishers.

Library of Congress Control Number: 2001012345

ISBN 0-8499-7723-1

Printed in the United States of America

01 02 03 04 05 PHX 5 4 3 2 1

CONTENTS

YOU ARE YOUNG,
BUT DO NOT LET ANYONE
TREAT YOU AS IF
YOU WERE NOT IMPORTANT.
BE AN EXAMPLE
TO SHOW THE BELIEVERS
HOW THEY SHOULD LIVE.
SHOW THEM WITH YOUR WORDS,
WITH THE WAY YOU LIVE,
WITH YOUR LOVE, WITH YOUR FAITH,
AND WITH YOUR PURE LIFE.

—1 TIMOTHY 4:12

Introduction

Leadership: Everyone talks about it, but few people really understand it. Everyone wants it, but few people achieve it. So what is leadership?

Most people would say that leadership is getting a title—like class president or team captain. They work and work to get the title, and when they do they think they are leaders instantly. But just because someone has the title of a leader, it doesn't mean people will follow him or her.

> He who thinketh he leadeth and hath no one following him is only taking a walk.

And then there are some leaders who don't even have a title. Think about certain kids in your class, the ones everyone looks to for how to dress, how to be cool. Or what about the people who may not dress as well, but their quiet intelligence or wit makes everyone want to follow them? They're all leaders, too.

So, What Is Leadership?

Leadership is influence—the ability to get people to follow you.

The goal of this journal is to prepare you to be a leader, both now and in the future. You'll look at how you influence others and how others influence you. You'll look at attitudes and problem solving, setting goals, and reaching goals. You'll have to do some thinking about who you are, who you want to be, and where you want to go. But when you reach the end, you'll have learned what it takes to be a good leader.

Why Me?

You may be asking *why* you should learn about leadership. That's because—in a big way or a small way—you *already* are a leader. Everyone is, because everyone influences the people around him. In fact, research has found that you will influence the lives of ten thousand other people in your lifetime. No matter whether you're shy or outgoing—ten thousand people! The question is *how* you will influence them. And that is up to you.

Think about the things that have influenced and changed you—maybe just for a day or maybe for your whole life. For example, have you ever had a run-in with a real grouch who just ruined the rest of your day? Or was there a special person who helped you decide that you wanted to be a Christian? Did you ever see a person do something incredible and then say, "That's what I want to do"? Influences can be big events, or they can be little, everyday things. Either way, they help to make you who you are.

Write about a big event or a special person who influenced your life.

_____

_____

_____

_____

_____

Write about a little event or a brief encounter with a person who influenced you.

_____
_____
_____
_____
_____
_____
_____
_____

Now, turn it around. Write about an event or person you influenced.

_____
_____
_____
_____
_____
_____

That's the power of influence—of leadership. You never know who or how much *you* influence someone. It's a big responsibility. And this journal will help you take it on.

There have been meetings of only a moment which have left impressions for life, for eternity. No one can understand that mysterious thing we call influence . . . yet . . . every one of us continually exerts influence, either to heal, to bless, to leave marks of beauty; or to wound, to hurt, to poison, to stain other lives.

—J. R. Miller

Making a Difference

The question is not whether you will influence someone. You *will* influence people. The question is whether you will be a good influence or a bad influence. Will you grow in your leadership skills? The primary goal of this journal is for you to:

Make a difference tomorrow by becoming a better leader today.

How do you want to make a difference?

You Can Learn Leadership

There are three basic levels of leadership—here we'll call them lockers. And with thought and practice, you can move from one locker up to the next.

Locker #1: You're in Charge!

This is the very basic leadership—because you have a title. Some people will follow you because you're in charge, but they'll follow you only so far before they stop. That's because real leadership requires more than a title; it requires trust and caring.

Locker #2: You're Cool

People have been watching you, and they're starting to think that you're pretty cool. They see that you really care about them. You spend time with them and try to find out more about what they want and need. People are beginning to trust you; they'll follow you a little farther now. They may even be willing to try something new. At the "You're Cool" level, people get together because they enjoy being together.

Leadership begins with the heart, not the head.

Locker #3: Make Things Happen

On this level things begin to happen—good things. Everyone is excited and eager to chip in and do their part, and get something done. They still enjoy just hanging out, but they *love* accomplishing something.

The Why and the Where

As you seek to become a better leader, keep in mind why you want to be a leader. Is it to help yourself or to help others? Write your answer below.

_____

_____

_____

_____

_____

_____

Now that that's settled, you've got to decide the most important question: *Where are you going to lead people?*

As a Christian, you know there is no better place to lead people than to Jesus Christ. And there are ways to do this, no matter what the project is at hand. For example, you may be in charge of putting together the homecoming float, and while that may seem like it has nothing to do with Jesus, your attitude and the way you treat people will be a powerful witness for Him.

> SO GO AND MAKE FOLLOWERS OF ALL PEOPLE IN THE WORLD. BAPTIZE THEM IN THE NAME OF THE FATHER AND THE SON AND THE HOLY SPIRIT.
> —MATTHEW 28:19

What are your thoughts? Where do you want to lead people?

_____

_____

_____

_____

_____

I KNOW, MY GOD, THAT YOU TEST PEOPLE'S HEARTS. YOU ARE HAPPY WHEN PEOPLE DO WHAT IS RIGHT.

—1 CHRONICLES 29:17

i

InteGRITy!?!

Earl didn't consider it cheating... he was simply making sure his answers were correct.

Who Am I When No One's Looking?

What's Integrity Anyway?

The dictionary defines *integrity* as "the state of being complete, unbroken." Okay, but what does that mean?

In a nutshell, *integrity* means doing and saying the right thing no matter who is watching—even if *no one* is watching! It means practicing what you preach. It means being honest with yourself and others about who you are. If you have integrity, you will be a "complete, unbroken" person because what you say and what you do match up.

Write about a time when someone told you he or she believed one thing, but you saw them do the opposite.

_____

_____

_____

_____

_____

_____

_____

_____

_____

How did that make you feel?

_____

_____

_____

Now be honest about yourself. Write about a time when you said one thing, but did another.

_____

_____

_____

_____

_____

How did you feel about yourself?

_____

_____

_____

If others had found out what you had done, how would you have felt?

_____

_____

_____

What Do I Need with Integrity?

Good question. In today's world, a lot of so-called leaders and role models don't have integrity. All you have to do is read a newspaper or watch television, and you'll see scandals about sports stars, movie stars, and even our country's highest leaders. If these people don't worry about having integrity, why should you?

The simplest—and best—answer is:

because Jesus had integrity.

As a Christian, your ultimate leader and role model is Jesus. And the best possible place that you can lead others is to Him. But people will follow you only if they trust you, and the first step toward getting people to trust you is doing what you say you will do. That's integrity, and that's worth having! And, more importantly, this will help others see Jesus in you.

If you weren't YOU, would you trust YOU?

List 10 Qualities That a Good LEADER Should Have.

1. _____

2. _____

3. _____

4. _____

5. _____

6. _____

7. _____

8. _____

9. _____

10. _____

HOW JESUS LED

Jesus knew that the Father had given him power over everything. He also knew that he had come from God and was going back to God. So during the meal Jesus stood up and took off his outer clothing. Taking a towel, he wrapped it around his waist. Then he poured water into a bowl and began to wash the followers' feet. He dried them with the towel that was wrapped around him. . . .

When he had finished washing their feet, he put on his clothes and sat down again. Jesus asked, "Do you understand what I have just done for you? You call me 'Teacher' and 'Lord.' And this is right, because that is what I am. I, your Lord and Teacher, have washed your feet. So you also should wash each other's feet. I did this as an example for you. So you should do as I have done for you."

—John 13:3–5, 12–15

What does this story tell you about Jesus as a leader?

_____

_____

_____

_____

Jesus led His disciples by showing them how He wanted them to act. He didn't just stand back and tell them what to do; He did it. The Bible is filled with examples of how Jesus led by doing and by serving. One such example is found in John 4. Jesus violates all the social codes of the day by not only speaking to a Samaritan woman, but one who has a shady reputation. Instead of shaming her, He offers her the living water of His truth. Another such example, in Mark 4, finds Jesus peacefully sleeping in the midst of a storm. When His disciples panic, Jesus calms the storm with a word, showing His disciples not only the power of the Lord, but the peace that can be found by trusting in Him.

List some of the qualities that made Jesus such a good leader.

_____

_____

_____

_____

How do Jesus' qualities compare to the ones you listed on page 5 that a good leader should have?

_____

_____

_____

_____

_____

_____

_____

_____

Think of a leader whom you admire. Write down the things that make this person a good leader.

_____

_____

_____

_____

_____

_____

_____

_____

_____

How does the way this person leads match up with the way Jesus led?

_____

_____

_____

_____

In the first column, list some of the things you do every day—go to school, help out at home, practice sports, baby-sit. In the next column, write down some ideas showing how you can both serve and lead others in these everyday situations—how you can lead from the lockers.

Everyday tasks

1. _____

2. _____

3. _____

4. _____

5. _____

6. _____

7. _____

8. _____

9. _____

Ways to serve and lead from the lockers

1. _____

2. _____

3. _____

4. _____

5. _____

6. _____

7. _____

8. _____

9. _____

Testing, Testing . . .
How's Your Integrity?

1. **Integrity means doing the right thing—whether you're alone or with a group. Are you the same person no matter who you are with?**

Your parents have talked to you about smoking, and you know how bad it is for you. You even gave a speech in health class about the dangers of smoking. But now you are at a concert with your friends. You've just met some kids from another school, and they are passing around a pack of cigarettes. Everyone is watching.

What do you do? What will your friends think if you take a cigarette? If you don't take one?

_____

_____

_____

_____

_____

2. **Integrity means doing the right thing**—_even when no one will ever know._

It's the final swim meet of the year, and you're up against your biggest rival. He lays his things on the bench and goes over to talk to some friends. He doesn't notice that his goggles have dropped back behind the bench, out of sight. You know he won't find them when he returns. You have a choice: You can leave them lying there, or you can pick them up and lay them with his other things.

''YOU MUST NOT DO WRONG JUST BECAUSE EVERYONE ELSE IS DOING IT.''
—**EXODUS 23:2**

What do you do?

_____

_____

_____

_____

_____

3. **Integrity means not doing the wrong thing**—_even when you won't get caught._

Your basketball coach is also your health teacher. At basketball practice, the coach realizes that she has left her playbook in her classroom, and she asks you to run get it for her. On her desk, you find the playbook—and a copy of tomorrow's big health test. No one will ever know if you just take a quick peek at it.

What do you do?

_____

_____

_____

_____

_____

_____

4. **Integrity means being honest**—*all the time.*

> BE HUMBLE AND GIVE
> MORE HONOR TO OTHERS
> THAN TO YOURSELVES.
> **—PHILIPPIANS 2:3**

An ace art student, you are asked to paint a mural of your school's mascot. It is a huge job, so you ask a friend from your art class to help. After the mural is finished, the principal presents you with a gift certificate to the mall for single-handedly doing such a great job.

What do you do?

_____

_____

_____

_____

_____

Upping Your Integrity

Step 1: It Starts with You

In some ways, life is like a battle, and integrity is your weapon. If you're always practicing integrity, you'll be ready when the real battle begins. Then you'll find that difficult decisions aren't so difficult.

But like any great warrior, you need to prepare for the battle now. Practice how you are going to act in difficult situations. What will you say? Say it out loud. Say it with conviction.

What kind of person would you like to be now?

_____

_____

_____

_____

_____

_____

_____

_____

_____

What kind of person would you like to be in ten years?

_____

_____

_____

_____

_____

_____

_____

What types of battles do you need to prepare for to reach your ten-year goal? (Stay in school? Keep away from drugs and alcohol? Remain close to your church? Talk over problems with your parents? Seek mentors?)

_____

_____

_____

_____

_____

_____

The next time you are faced with a difficult decision—one that affects integrity—look back at what you've written. You may find that you have already made the decision and decided how to handle the problem.

Step 2: Be Someone to Count On

There are some people you can always count on. You know, that one person whom you can always turn to, no matter what. Maybe it's your mom or dad, a teacher, your youth leader at church, or a best friend. You can count on that person to be there for you, to do whatever he says he will do. That is a person of integrity.

> I KNOW THAT YOU NEED ME, AND SO I KNOW THAT I WILL STAY WITH YOU.
> —PHILIPPIANS 1:25

You can be someone to count on, too. It's really very simple. Do what you say you will do. Don't leave things unfinished. When you promise to help someone, do it. Pretty soon, people will turn to you because they know that you are someone to count on.

Think of someone whom you count on. How do you know you can count on that person?

_____

_____

_____

_____

_____

_____

List Some Ways You Can Be Counted On

1. _____

2. _____

3. _____

4. _____

5. _____

6. _____

7. _____

8. _____

9. _____

10. _____

11. _____

12. _____

13. _____

14. _____

15. _____

The flip side of this coin is knowing what to do when someone you've counted on lets you down. Everyone makes mistakes. At some time you, too, will make a mistake.

What will you do when someone lets you down?

_____

_____

_____

_____

_____

Write about a time when you let someone down.

_____

_____

_____

_____

_____

How did you want to be treated by that person?

_____

_____

_____

_____

_____

Step 3: Copycat, Copycat

By nature, people are copycats—they do whatever they see other people doing. So the question is: When you're out there at the lockers, what do people see you doing? Remember that as a leader, people will be looking for your integrity—checking to see if what you say matches what you do. If it doesn't, they won't follow you for very long.

At church on Sunday morning, Sarah helps to teach the lesson in her Sunday school class. She talks about how important it is to be kind and helpful to everyone because that's what Jesus would do.

Emily has come with Sarah to church. She isn't a Christian, but as she listens to what Sarah and the others say she becomes interested. Then at the lockers on Monday, Emily sees Sarah making fun of the new student because his clothes are so different. And later at softball practice, Emily overhears Sarah gossiping to the others about a girl who is having trouble with her boyfriend.

How do you think Emily will feel about Christians now?

_____

_____

_____

_____

_____

_____

people do what people see.

What do people see you doing?

What are some areas that you need to work on? (Not gossiping? Being kind to everyone? Doing what you say you will do?)

_____

_____

_____

_____

_____

What steps can you take to help yourself in these areas that you wrote about above?

_____

_____

_____

_____

Step 4: Just Trust Me . . .

A person with integrity is not two-faced—saying one thing to one person and another thing to someone else. And a person with integrity is not phony, pretending to be someone that she isn't—that's called being a hypocrite.

Sadly, some people work harder on how they appear on the outside than how they are on the inside. But sooner or later, people will *always* see you for who you really are—not just who you say you are. And if who you are is very different from who you *say* you are, then no one will trust you. And if no one trusts you, no one will follow you.

> IN YOUR LIVES YOU MUST THINK AND ACT LIKE CHRIST JESUS.
> —PHILIPPIANS 2:5

We all know people who are not the same on the inside as they are on the outside. Think of someone you know who is like that.

Do you enjoy being around this person? Do you trust him or her? Is this a person you want to be like?

_____

_____

_____

_____

Are there some things about you that are "phony"?

_____

_____

_____

_____

_____

_____

What will you do to fix them?

_____

_____

_____

_____

_____

_____

Phonies are always found out!

Freedom!

Integrity gives you freedom. How? Well, for one thing, you have fewer things to worry about. If what you say and what you do match up, then you have nothing to hide. You don't have to worry about getting caught or having a secret "found out."

> DOING WHAT IS RIGHT PROTECTS THE HONEST PERSON.
> —PROVERBS 13:6

And if you aren't two-faced, then you don't have to worry about remembering whom you said what to.

Think about a time when you were less than honest and kind. Perhaps you didn't tell your parents the whole truth about something that happened at school. Or perhaps you said something hurtful about a friend behind his back.

When it was all over, how did you feel about yourself?

_____

_____

_____

_____

_____

Integrity helps you make decisions. There will always be things that you want to do, even though you know you really shouldn't. But when you know what you believe, and you are determined to do the right thing, difficult decisions become easier.

Allen, a guy in your class, is having a party. Your parents say you can go, but they don't know that Allen's parents are out of town. You think the party might get a little wild. You've heard that there was some drinking at Allen's last party. Do you go?

How do you explain your choice to your friends? Your parents?

_____

_____

_____

_____

_____

_____

Integrity helps you know when to say "No" and when to say "Yes."

This Integrity Stuff Is Hard Work!

Integrity isn't always easy. It takes hard work, self-discipline, and complete honesty with yourself and others. But the rewards are terrific. Not only will other people trust you to lead them, but when you look in the mirror, you'll like the person staring back at you.

What is most important to you in life?

_____

_____

_____

_____

_____

_____

_____

_____

_____

_____

_____

_____

FOLLOW MY EXAMPLE,
AS I FOLLOW THE
EXAMPLE OF CHRIST.
    —1 CORINTHIANS 11:1

Ask someone who knows you well what areas of your life she sees as consistent (you do what you say) and what areas she sees as inconsistent (you say but you don't always do what you say).

What will you do to fix these problem areas?

_____

_____

_____

_____

_____

_____

The Integrity Checklist

☐   Say what you mean.

☐   Do what you say.

☐   Be honest with others.

☐   Put what is best for others ahead of what is best for you.

☐   Don't be a phony!

Myself

I have to live with myself, and so
I want to be fit for myself to know,
I want to be able, as days go by,
Always to look myself straight in the eye;
I don't want to stand, with the setting sun,
And hate myself for things I have done.
I don't want to keep on a closet shelf
A lot of secrets about myself. . .
. . . .
I can never hide myself from me;
I see what others may never see;
I know what others may never know,
I never can fool myself, and so,
Whatever happens, I want to be
Self-respecting and conscience free.

—Edgar Guest

Write a prayer asking God to help you become a person of integrity.

_____

_____

_____

_____

_____

VISION IS THE LIGHT
THAT KEEPS YOU HEADED
DOWN THE RIGHT PATH
WHEN ALL THE WORLD
AROUND YOU
IS DARK.

2
What's a "Vision"?

It's hard to hit goals you can't see.

Setting the Goals
To Get Where I Wanna Go

The Light at the End of the Tunnel

Vision can be defined as the light at the end of the tunnel. It's the light that keeps you headed down the right path when all the world around you is dark. Vision is the big picture; it's where you want to go. In simple terms, it's your dream, your goal.

The first rule of leadership is to know *where* you are going to lead people. And that begins with knowing where you are going to lead yourself—what your vision is.

But how do you know what your vision is? Does it drop out of the sky and hit you on the head? Do you look in the newspaper or on the Internet want ads for one? Is it buried somewhere in the back of your locker, maybe under last week's gym socks?

Nope. Visions don't fall out of the sky, and you won't find them in the newspaper or even in cyberspace. And while there might be something buried under those gym socks, it's probably not a vision.

A vision is something you create for yourself. It's tailor-made *for* you, *by* you. To create a vision, you first need to know a few things about yourself, about who you want to be, and about what you want to do.

Helen Keller was asked,

"What would be worse than being born blind?"

She replied,

"To have sight without vision."

What's your definition of vision?

_____

_____

_____

_____

_____

_____

_____

_____

_____

_____

If you don't know where you're going, you'll end up someplace.
—Yogi Berra

Time to Think

Creating your own vision starts with you. This is the time to do some serious thinking about yourself.

What are your hopes, your dreams, your goals?

These questions and a hundred others will keep popping up throughout your life. It's enough to make your head spin! But—believe it or not—creating a vision for your life now will make these questions easier to answer in the future. That doesn't mean your vision won't ever change, but you will have some idea of where you want to go and why.

More than likely, you'll have more than one vision. After all, in a way, there's more than one you. Think about it; everyone has lots of different roles in life. You're a son or daughter, a brother or sister, a student at school, a member of your church youth group, a basketball player, and so on. You might have a different vision—a different place you want to go—for each of these areas of your life.

Make a List of All the Different Roles You Have

1. _____
2. _____
3. _____
4. _____
5. _____
6. _____
7. _____
8. _____
9. _____
10. _____
11. _____
12. _____
13. _____
14. _____
15. _____

Look back at your list. More than likely, most of your roles will fit into one of five categories: Spiritual Life, Family Life, School and Future Career, Personal Life (such as friendships, sports, or hobbies), and Other Stuff. Each of these areas of your life is a big part of who you are today. Now, let's take a look at how to create a vision for each of these areas.

Dreaming the Dream

Now is the time to really do some dreaming—big dreaming. As you begin to create your own vision, first look to these five places for ideas:

above you
    inside you
        around you
            beside you
                ahead of you

What you see
IS
what you can be.

1. Look above You: What Does God Want You to Do?

As a child of God, this is the very best place for you to start. What does God want you to do with your life? Pray about this, think about this, and then answer the following questions.

What does God want you to do in your spiritual life?

_____

_____

_____

What does God want you to do in your family life?

_____

_____

_____

What does God want you to do at school and in your future career?

_____

_____

_____

What does God want from you in your personal life?

MY GOD,
I WANT TO DO WHAT YOU
WANT. YOUR TEACHINGS
ARE IN MY HEART.
—PSALM 40:8

_____

_____

_____

_____

_____

_____

_____

_____

Is there any "other stuff" that God wants you to do?

_____

_____

_____

_____

_____

_____

_____

_____

God's gift to me is my potential. My gift back to God is what I do with that potential.

Write a prayer asking God to show you His will for your life.

_____

_____

_____

_____

_____

_____

Over time, your visions and dreams may change. But no matter what your dreams are, always take time to pray and make sure they are in line with what God wants. You will never truly be successful unless you do.

What is your definition of success?

_____

_____

_____

_____

_____

_____

_____

What do you need to feel like a success?

_____

_____

_____

_____

TEACH ME
TO DO WHAT YOU WANT,
BECAUSE YOU ARE
MY GOD.

—PSALM 143:10

_____

_____

_____

_____

The world defines *success* in a lot of ways—how much money you have, how famous you are, how many people listen to you. But a better definition of success is:

Knowing God and what He wants for me.
Becoming the very best person I can be.
Doing things that help others.

What a terrible waste of life
to be climbing the ladder of success
only to find when you reach the top
that you were leaning against
the wrong building!

2. Look inside You

What are your secret hopes and dreams? What would you like to do most? If you had all the time, all the money, everything you could ever possibly want or need, what would you do? Wow! Just think of the possibilities!

Great visions begin as an "inside job."

Now, you may say that you don't have everything you need to make your dreams come true, but don't let that stop you. Thomas Edison was partially deaf and thought to be "slow," yet he became a great inventor. Champion cyclist Lance Armstrong beat seemingly inpossible odds in his struggle with cancer and went on to win the awesome Tour de France not once, but twice. In fact, many famous people began their lives in the poorest of homes, with little education and impossible odds, yet became successful.

Think of a person whom you consider successful. Why do you consider that person successful?

_____

_____

_____

_____

_____

The amazing thing about Abraham Lincoln was not that he was born in a log cabin, but that he made it out of that log cabin and to the White House!

What can you learn about success and achieving your vision from this person?

_____

_____

_____

DON'T BE AFRAID TO DREAM BIG!

Many years ago, a bishop from the East Coast paid a visit to a small religious college. He stayed at the home of the college president, who also served as professor of physics and chemistry. After dinner the bishop declared that the millennium (the 1900 one!) couldn't be far off, because just about everything about nature had been discovered and everything that could be invented already had been.

The young college president politely disagreed and said he felt there would be many more discoveries. When the angry bishop challenged the president to name just one such invention, the president replied he was certain that within fifty years men would be able to fly.

"Nonsense!" sputtered the outraged bishop. "Only angels were meant to fly!"

It so happened that the sputtering bishop's name was Wright, and he had two boys at home who would prove to have greater vision than their father. Their names were Orville and Wilbur. The father and his sons both lived under the same sky, but they didn't have the same horizon!

—adapted from A Savior for All Seasons *by William Barker*

What does this story tell you about vision?

_____

_____

_____

Now it's time for you to dream—to create the biggest and best
vision you can. Remember, it doesn't matter if your vision
seems impossible or maybe even a little silly to others. It's your
vision, your dream—it can be anything you want it to be!

If I could do anything in my spiritual life, I would . . .

_____

_____

_____

If I could do anything in my family life, I would . . .

_____

_____

_____

Hitch your wagon to a star.

—Ralph Waldo Emerson

If I could do anything in my school life, I would . . .

_____

_____

_____

_____

_____

Keep your eyes
on the stars,
and your feet
on the ground.

—Theodore Roosevelt

If I could do anything in my
personal life, I would . . .

_____

_____

_____

_____

_____

_____

If I could do anything in my future career life, I would . . .

_____

_____

_____

_____

_____

Other dreams I would like to make come true . . .

_____

_____

_____

_____

_____

_____

3. Look around You: What Does the World Need?

What is your vision for the world around you? What *needs* to be done? Is there a particular part of your spiritual life that you are struggling with? A relationship in your family that needs to be better? A subject in school you need to work extra hard on? Perhaps someone in your church who could be helped by your youth group? Remember, if you're going to lead from the lockers (from where you are), it's best to take a look around at what those kids around the lockers really need.

What needs to be done to make the world a better place?

_____

_____

_____

_____

_____

What can you do to help make these things happen?

_____

_____

_____

_____

_____

_____

_____

_____

_____

4. Look beside You: What Is Happening to Others?

Think about the different areas of your life, once again. Who are the other people involved? What are their visions and dreams, their worries and concerns? How can you help them, and how can they help you? Do they have some problems or worries that you need to deal with before you can try to reach your goals? For example, if you just had a huge fight with your sister, you will need to make peace with her so that you can restore unity in your family.

Make a list of the people involved in all the areas of your life. These should be the people who can help you with your dreams, and those whom you can help with their dreams.

The people in my family life, and how we can help each other. . .

_____

_____

_____

_____

_____

_____

_____

_____

_____

The people in my school and future career life, and how we can help each other. . .

_____

_____

_____

_____

_____

_____

_____

_____

_____

_____

_____

_____

The people in my personal life, and how we can help each
other. . .

_____

_____

_____

_____

_____

_____

_____

_____

Other people whom I can reach out to, and how we can help
each other. . .

_____

_____

_____

_____

_____

_____

_____

_____

5. Look Ahead of You: What Is the Big Picture?

Your vision and goals for tomorrow may be different from those for next year, which may be different from those for ten years from now, which may be different from . . . well, you get the idea. And it's okay to change. That's all part of growing up.

On the next few pages, write down your goals, your vision for this week, this year, for after high school, and for your life in general. There's extra space so that you can come back later and make changes and additions whenever you want.

My Spiritual Life . . .

Goals for this week:

_____

_____

_____

Goals for this year:

_____

_____

_____

_____

My Family Life . . .
Goals for this week:

_____

_____

_____

Goals for this year:

_____

_____

_____

_____

My School and Future Career Life . . .
Goals for after high school:

_____

_____

_____

Goals for my life:

_____

_____

_____

_____

My Personal Life . . .
Goals for after high school:

_____

_____

_____

Goals for my life:

_____

_____

_____

_____

My Other Goals . . .
Goals for this year:

_____

_____

_____

Goals for my life:

_____

_____

_____

_____

You see things;
and you say
"Why?" But I
dream things that
never were; and I
say "Why not?"

—George Bernard Shaw

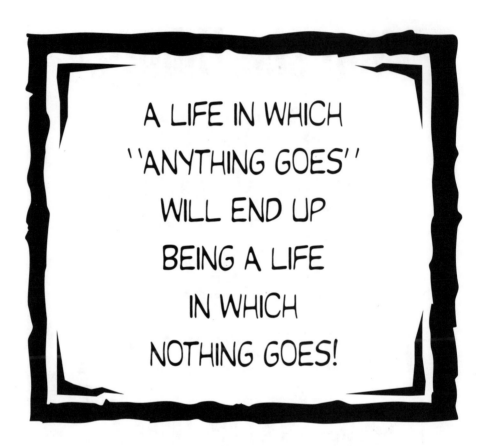

A LIFE IN WHICH
''ANYTHING GOES''
WILL END UP
BEING A LIFE
IN WHICH
NOTHING GOES!

3

First Things First

How to Get It All Done

(Now That I Know What I Wanna Do!)

The Three-Ring Circus

Does it ever seem like everything happens all at once? Your team's biggest game of the year is this weekend, which means extra practice time; you have a book report due in English class and a huge test in math; it's your brother's birthday; and your youth group is heading off on this great canoeing trip that you really don't want to miss—and there's still all the everyday stuff like school and church and chores. *Yikes!*

Times like these can make life feel like a three-ring circus—and you're the star juggler! Being able to juggle three or four big things at once is an important skill. The trick is in knowing where to start, which things to juggle, and which things to put down for a while. With a little practice and a little organization, you'll be a pro in no time.

Think of a time when you had three or four big things happening all at once. What did you do? Did everything go the way you wanted?

_____

_____

_____

_____

_____

Work Smart

It's not only important to work hard, but it is also important to work smart!

> A man was told that if he worked the very hardest he could, he would become rich. Well, the hardest work the man knew was digging holes, so he set about digging great holes in his backyard. He didn't get rich; he only got a backache. He worked hard, but he didn't work smart.

There are two keys to working smart: think ahead and put first things first.

What do you think it means to work smart?

_____

_____

_____

Have you ever worked "dumb"? What were the results?

_____

_____

_____

1. Think Ahead

Surprises can be a lot of fun—surprise parties, surprise guests, surprise snow days. But some surprises aren't fun. Like remembering that your book report on *Huckleberry Finn* is due *this* Wednesday, not next Wednesday! But if you think ahead you can avoid many of the not-so-nice surprises. A good way to do this is to keep a calendar or notebook handy. Jot down things you need to remember, such as homework assignments, practice times, get-togethers with friends, special birthdays, and other important stuff—and then—and this is really important—remember to look at it every day and check today's schedule *and* the next couple of days' as well.

Below, jot down all the things you have coming up in the next week. Include everything, no matter how small.

To Do

1. _____
2. _____
3. _____
4. _____
5. _____
6. _____
7. _____
8. _____
9. _____
10. _____

11. _____
12. _____
13. _____
14. _____
15. _____
16. _____
17. _____
18. _____
19. _____
20. _____

2. Put First Things First

The ability to put first things first—to prioritize your responsibilities—is the second key to working smart. Sometimes this means choosing what to do first, and sometimes this means choosing what not to do at all.

The Good, the Bad, and the Ugly

Some choices are obviously good—going backpacking with your friends, practicing your hook shot, volunteering to help at church. Some choices are obviously bad—renting an R-rated movie behind your parents' backs, lying on the couch and watching television for the entire weekend, skipping class

> THIS IS MY PRAYER FOR YOU:
> . . . THAT YOU WILL SEE THE DIFFERENCE BETWEEN GOOD AND BAD AND CHOOSE THE GOOD.
> **—PHILIPPIANS 1:9-10**

to go to the mall. And some choices are just plain ugly — doing drugs, drinking alcohol, or having sex before marriage. When it comes to the good, the bad, and the ugly, your choices are pretty clear.

Have you made any bad choices lately? What should you have done differently?

_____

_____

_____

_____

If you have made—or are thinking of making—any ugly choices, write down the names of some people you can talk to about them—like a parent, a counselor at church or school, even a good friend.

And then go talk to that person right away!

_____

_____

_____

_____

Decide what to do and do it; decide what not to do and don't do it.

Good, Better, Best

Sometimes the choice isn't between a good thing and a bad thing. Sometimes you have to choose between two good things. For example, your friend's dad has offered to take you and some other kids rock climbing this weekend; your mom also has promised to take you shopping for some new clothes this weekend. They are both good things, but which one do you do?

THERE IS A RIGHT TIME FOR EVERYTHING.
—ECCLESIASTES 3:1

Here are some tips for breaking the tie between two good things.

1. **Try to figure out a way to do one of the things at another time.** Ask your mom if you can go shopping another day, so that you can still go rock climbing with your friend's dad and the other kids.

2. **Can someone else help you out?**

Abby is supposed to help take up the tickets at the ball game Friday night, but her family is having a huge party for her grandmother's seventieth birthday that same night. Abby knows that Jarred is supposed to take up the tickets at next week's game, so she asks him to trade nights with her, and he agrees. Now, Abby can go to her grandmother's party, while still making sure that her responsibilities are covered.

3. Look at which thing best fits with your goals for the future.

> Camille would like to start baby-sitting for money. The Red Cross is offering a baby-sitting certification class this weekend. But Camille also has a chance to go to the movies with her friends that day. After some thought, she chooses the Red Cross class because it better fits her goals—and she knows she can spend time with her friends later.

4. Ask your parents or your friends for their opinion. They may come up with a solution you would have never considered.

It's easy to get overloaded. So, when you have too many things to do, try writing them all down and then examining them using the tips above. Remember, it's okay to say "No"— even to a good thing.

Write about some times you have had to choose between two good things. How did you choose what to do?

_____

_____

_____

_____

_____

_____

Whadya Do When There's Too Much to Do?

Hurry, hurry, hurry! Get up, get going, go to school, finish your homework, get to practice, call so-and-so—some days there's just too much for one person to do. How will you ever get it all done?

No one can do everything, so take a look at these three tips for deciding what to do and what not to do.

1. What are the things that you absolutely must do?

Look back at your "To Do" list from earlier in the chapter. What do you absolutely have to do? Write down everything that *must* be done in the next week. (This includes chores, homework, church, sports practices—and be sure to add some time for yourself.) Also, beside each item, note about how long it will take you to complete it.

	To Do	Time It Will Take
1.	_____	_____
2.	_____	_____
3.	_____	_____
4.	_____	_____
5.	_____	_____
6.	_____	_____
7.	_____	_____
8.	_____	_____

2. If you had time, what would you like to do?

Make a list of these things, also.

1. _____

2. _____

3. _____

4. _____

5. _____

6. _____

7. _____

8. _____

9. _____

10. _____

3. Which things can you postpone or skip completely, if you have to?

List these things here.

1. _____

2. _____

3. _____

4. _____

5. _____

Putting It All Together

Now that you've gotten everything written down, it's time to put it all in order. Look at all the things you have to do in the next week and write them on the calendar below. Add in as many of the things that you would like to do as you can. Remember also to allow yourself some "downtime"—time to spend with God, to daydream, or to just do nothing.

Must Do	Want to Do	Other Stuff to Remember
SUN. _____	_____	_____
_____	_____	_____
_____	_____	_____
MON. _____	_____	_____
_____	_____	_____
_____	_____	_____
TUES. _____	_____	_____
_____	_____	_____
_____	_____	_____
WED. _____	_____	_____
_____	_____	_____
_____	_____	_____

	Must Do	Want to Do	Other Stuff to Remember
THUR.			
FRI.			
SAT.			

Write down a couple of emergencies that have popped up for you and explain how you dealt with them.

_____

_____

_____

_____

_____

_____

_____

Would you do things differently now?

_____

_____

_____

_____

_____

Emergency! Emergency!

Just when you think you've got it all figured out, up pops an emergency. A test announced at the last minute, an unexpected weekend trip with your parents, a last-minute soccer practice. But that's okay. That's just part of life. Take care of your emergency project, then get back to your regular schedule as best you can.

Write a prayer asking God to help you use your time wisely.

_____

_____

_____

_____

_____

DO EVERYTHING WITHOUT COMPLAINING OR ARGUING.

—PHILIPPIANS 2:14

4
But I Don't Wanna!

How to Get the Right Attitude

I Don't Feel Like It

How many times have you said, "But I don't feel like it"? You know you should do it; it's the right thing to do—like you really should spend more prayer time with God, you really should be nicer to your brother, you really should make an extra effort to be friends with that new kid in karate class.

But you just don't wanna. It's easier not to.

List some things that you know you should do, but you just don't wanna.

_____

_____

_____

_____

_____

_____

_____

_____

_____

The good news is that there is a huge difference between how you feel and how you *choose* to handle those feelings—and that difference is ATTITUDE.

Your attitude is your most important asset. It determines how you see things and how you handle your feelings. And these two things greatly determine how successful you will be in life and in leadership.

Write the name of a friend whom you admire.

_____

Write down the one thing you admire most about that friend.

_____

_____

_____

_____

Chances are that the thing you admire most about your friend has something to do with his or her attitude.

See What You Wanna See . . .

       Do What You Wanna Do . . .

              Be Who You Wanna Be . . .

WHAT HAPPENED?

The principal of a school called three teachers together and said, "Because you three teachers are the best in our school, we're going to give you ninety of the brightest students. We're going to let you move these students through this next year at their own pace and see how much they can learn."

The teachers and students were thrilled.

Over the next year the teachers and students thoroughly enjoyed themselves. The teachers were teaching the brightest students; the students had the best teachers. By the end of the year, the students had achieved from 20 to 30 percent more than the other students in the school.

The principal called the teachers in later and told them, "I have a confession to make. You did not have the ninety brightest students; they were just average students."

The teachers said, "This means that we must really be great teachers."

But the principal said, "I have another confession. You're not the best of the teachers. Your names were just the first three names drawn out of a hat."

The teachers asked, "What made the difference? Why did ninety students do so well for a whole year?"

—*adapted from* Beliefs Can Influence Attitudes, *by Nell Mohney*

What do you think made the difference?

_____

_____

_____

_____

_____

_____

_____

_____

What's the answer? The difference, of course, was the teachers' expectations—and the students' expectations, too. Expectations have a great deal to do with attitudes.

Expect to be the best — and you will be!

The flip side of this is that even when your expectations are wrong, they can shape your attitude.

An older gentleman, unable to find his best saw, suspected that his neighbor's son—who was always tinkering around with woodworking—had stolen it. During the next week, everything the teenager did looked suspicious and sneaky—the way he walked, the things he said, even the way he waved across the yard. But when the older man found the saw behind his own workbench, where he had accidentally knocked it, he could no longer see anything at all sneaky about his neighbor's son.

What does this tell you about wrong expectations and attitudes?

It's Your Choice

Everyone has a bad day once in a while—sometimes even a few bad days in a row. And while having a good attitude won't stop you from having a bad day, it can keep your bad day from stopping you!

A BAD DAY?

Josh rolled over and burrowed under the covers to escape the light his mom had just turned on.

"Josh, you're going to be late for school. It's past time to get up," she called.

Josh groaned and turned to look at the clock. 7:15! How could that be? Why didn't the alarm go off at 6:30 like it was supposed to?

Twenty minutes later, Josh ran out the door, his backpack dragging and his jacket flapping—just in time to see the school bus disappear around the corner. Just great, he thought.

Josh made it to school and slid into his seat just before the tardy bell rang. Whew!

"Okay, class, take out your paper and pencils. We're having a pop quiz on last night's homework. And pass your homework to the front."

Could this day get any worse? Josh dug into his backpack for a paper and pencil, only to realize that his day had just, in fact, gotten worse—he didn't have last night's homework. It was still sitting on his desk at home. He'd been in such a hurry, he'd forgotten to get it.

Josh survived the test and the rest of the morning. But lunch was mystery meat with some kind of gravy that wound up all over his shirt.

Josh's afternoon classes went okay, but wrestling practice was embarrassing. Right away he got pinned twice—and in front of Jessica, the girl he secretly liked. At last, he made it home. As he walked in the door, his mom asked how his day had been.

If you were Josh, what would you say?

What if you knew a little bit more about Josh's day? For example, what if you knew that when Josh missed the bus, he caught a ride to school with his dad? They had a terrific time making plans for their camping trip the next weekend.

In class, Josh aced the pop quiz. And, after Josh explained about leaving his homework, the teacher agreed to let him bring it in the next day.

The mystery meat at lunch will probably always be a mystery, but the brownie for dessert was pretty good. And while Jessica saw Josh get pinned twice in wrestling practice, she also saw him win two other matches and tie a third.

Now, how would you say Josh's day was?

_____

_____

_____

_____

_____

_____

See, it's your choice. You can choose to only think about the things that went wrong—to have a bad attitude. Or you can choose to think about the things that went right—to have a good attitude.

Which would you rather do? Why?

_____

_____

_____

_____

_____   THE WORLD IS FULL OF HAPPINESS, AND

_____   PLENTY TO GO ROUND, IF YOU ARE ONLY

                       WILLING TO TAKE THE KIND THAT COMES

_____   YOUR WAY. THE WHOLE SECRET IS IN BEING

                       PLIABLE.

_____   **—FROM *DADDY-LONGLEGS* BY JEAN WEBSTER**

73

Now think about this: Would you rather be around someone who has a bad attitude and only talks about the things that go wrong? Or would you rather spend time with someone who has a good attitude? Why?

_____

_____

_____

_____

_____

_____

_____

Think about a bad day you've had recently. Now, write down some good things that happened that day, also.

_____

_____

_____

_____

_____

_____

_____

If you think you are beaten, you are.

If you think you dare not, you don't.

If you'd like to win but think you can't,

It's almost certain you won't.

Life's battles don't always go

To the stronger or faster,

But sooner or later, the one who wins

Is the one who thinks he can.

Excuses, Excuses

It's a fact: Life is full of surprises. Anything could happen—your alarm clock doesn't go off, you get a new baby brother, your parents get a divorce, and so on and so forth. Because life is always changing, you have to keep changing your attitude. And it won't change all by itself; you have to *make* it change.

It's up to you—you choose what attitude you will have. It's amazing how many people—grownups and kids alike—won't take responsibility for their attitudes. When things don't go their way, they'll say things like, "I got up on the wrong side of the bed," "I was born on the wrong side of the tracks," or "I was in the wrong place at the wrong time."

Notice something? They are making excuses. Blaming everyone else for their problems.

What do you think about people who make excuses?

_____

_____

_____

_____

_____

_____

You will truly be a grownup when you take responsibility for your attitude.

List some of the excuses you've heard—or even given yourself.

_____

_____

_____

_____

_____

_____

What does the poem on page 75 mean to you?

_____

_____

_____

_____

_____

_____

What are some things in your life that you can control? How will you choose to think about them?

_____

_____

_____

_____

What are some things that are out of your control? How will you choose to think about them?

_____

_____

_____

_____

We cannot choose how many years we will live,
*   but we can choose how much life those years will have.*
We cannot control the beauty of our face,
*   but we can control the expression on it.*
We cannot control life's difficult moments,
*   but we can choose to make life less difficult.*
We cannot control the negative atmosphere of the world,
*   but we can control the atmosphere of our minds.*
Too often, we try to choose and control things we cannot.
Too seldom, we choose to control what we can . . .
*   our attitude.*

—Anonymous

Misery Is an Option

SHARING AN ATTITUDE

There was a woman who went Christmas shopping with her daughter. The stores were packed with people. The woman had to skip lunch because she was in a hurry. She was tired and hungry, and her feet were hurting. She was more than a little grouchy.

As they left the last store, she asked her daughter, "Did you see the nasty look that salesman gave me?"

The daughter answered, "He didn't give it to you, Mom. You had it when you went in."

Has your bad attitude ever rubbed off on someone else?

_____

_____

_____

_____

How could you have handled things better?

_____

_____

_____

_____

It's not what happens TO me that matters but what happens IN me.

You can't control how other people will treat you, but you can control how you react to them. And sometimes, returning a bad attitude with kindness can make the other person change his or her attitude.

Can you remember a time when someone else's bad attitude rubbed off on you?

_____

_____

_____

_____

How should you have reacted?

_____

_____

_____

_____

The Happiness Condition

"DO FOR OTHER PEOPLE THE SAME THINGS YOU WANT THEM TO DO FOR YOU."
—MATTHEW 7:12

A lot of people seem to believe that happiness just happens. When good things happen to them, they are happy. When bad things happen to them, they are sad.

And there are the people who have "Someone Sickness." They'd be so happy if only this certain person would be their friend, sit next to them at lunch, choose them for her team, ask them to the party.

Other people have "Destination Disease." They'd be so happy if only they would get to go to rock-climbing camp, be elected class president, get to play starting point guard on the basketball team.

The problem with this kind of thinking is that things don't always go the way you want them to go. What then? Do you just go around being miserable, and making everyone around you miserable? Or do you choose to find other things to be happy about?

"THOSE WHO WANT TO DO RIGHT MORE THAN ANYTHING ELSE ARE HAPPY."
—MATTHEW 5:6

Write about a time when you had "Someone Sickness" or "Destination Disease."

_____

_____

_____

_____

_____

_____

When you got what you thought would make you happy, were you as happy as you thought you would be?

_____

_____

_____

_____

_____

How long did the happiness last?

_____

_____

_____

_____

_____

When It's Hard to Be Happy

Many times people who have had a terrible experience in their lives become bitter and angry. Their whole life becomes negative, and they are cold toward others. They point back to that terrible time in their lives and say, "That ruined my life." What they do not realize is that the terrible time called for a choice—an attitude choice. And they chose to be bitter. It was their wrong attitude choice—not the terrible experience—that really ruined their lives.

Think about Helen Keller. She was blind, deaf, and mute. But this is what she had to say about it:

> Blindness is an exciting business, I tell you; if you don't believe it, get up some dark night on the wrong side of your bed when the house is on fire and try to find the door.

Helen Keller had a sense of humor about the problems in life. How could a sense of humor help you to get through a difficult time?

_____

_____

_____

_____

_____

A GOOD CHOICE OR A BAD CHOICE?

Clara Barton, the founder of the American Red Cross, understood the importance of choosing a right attitude even in wrong situations. She was never known to hold a grudge against anyone. A friend once recalled to her a cruel thing that had happened to her some years previously, but Clara seemed not to remember the incident.

"Don't you remember the wrong that was done to you?" the friend asked.

"No," Clara answered calmly. "I distinctly remember forgetting that."

Is there something—big or small—that you're feeling bitter about? Write what happened here. Are you going to keep feeling bitter or will you choose to forget about it?

_____

_____

_____

_____

_____

_____

_____

_____

_____

Catching the Attitude Cold

The people around you can catch your attitude just as easily as they can catch your cold—just by getting close to you. Give a smile, and many smiles will be given back to you. Give an angry word, and many angry words will be given back to you.

Think about the people you enjoy being around. Do they give away smiles or angry words?

_____

_____

_____

_____

_____

SMILE,
and the whole world smiles with you.

The Smile Survey

Try this. Take a day and go to the mall or another place where you'll see a lot of people. For the first part of the day, smile at everyone you pass.

How many people smiled back at you?

_____

_____

For the next part of the day, still look at the people you pass but don't smile.

How many smiles did you get this time?

_____

_____

What does this tell you about how contagious your attitude can be?

_____

_____

Write a goal for yourself dealing with how you will try to greet other people from now on.

_____

_____

Positively Impossible

When things seem impossible, it can be hard to keep a positive attitude. But what seems impossible today may be possible tomorrow.

THE FOUR-MINUTE MILE

Ever heard of the four-minute mile? People had been trying to run a mile in four minutes since the days of the ancient Greeks. In fact, the Greeks even tried having lions chase the runners, thinking that would make them run faster. They also tried drinking tiger's milk. But nothing worked. So they decided it was impossible for a person to run a mile in four minutes or less. And for more than a thousand years, everyone believed it. The experts said that the human bone structure was all wrong. Wind resistance was too great. Humans didn't have enough lung power. There were a million reasons.

Then a man named Roger Bannister proved everyone wrong; he ran the four-minute mile. And then, miracle of miracles, the next year thirty-seven other runners broke the four-minute mile. The year after that, three hundred runners broke the four-minute mile.

What happened? There were no great breakthroughs in training. No one discovered how to control wind resistance. Human bone structure and lung power didn't suddenly improve—but human attitudes did.

List some goals that seem impossible right now. What can you do to make them possible?

_____

_____

_____

_____

_____

It does not matter if they say you can't do it. The ONLY thing that matters is if YOU say you can't do it.

Clean Up Your Attitude

Gotta hurry. Your friends are coming over in just a few minutes, but your room is a mess. Just shove everything in the closet and shut the door. Now, your room looks great! That's all that matters, right?

Whoops! Someone accidentally opened your closet door. Out come the dirty clothes, the candy bar wrappers, and last semester's art project. Sure, your room looked great on the outside, but it wasn't really clean.

That's exactly what people do in their lives. They spend a lot of time, money, and energy to look great on the outside. They have the latest fashions, the hot new hairstyles, the perfect look. But inside, their attitudes are all yucky. And sooner or later, those yucky attitudes will come spilling out.

But bad attitudes can be changed by:

Thinking right,
Doing right,
Feeling right.

Thinking Right

Think about the things you know you should be doing, about the kind of person you want to be. Write your thoughts here.

_____

_____

_____

_____

_____

_____

_____

_____

Doing Right

Now, just do it. Start doing all those things you know you should do. Start acting like the person you want to be. Don't wait until you feel like it; that will come later.

So, make a plan. Write it down. Put reminder notes to yourself on your mirror and in your school locker. Tell your family and friends about your plan and get them to help you. And when you find yourself slipping back into that bad attitude, read the Bible—God's Word is the best encourager of all.

Write your plan to "do right" here.

Feeling Right

Feelings follow action. It sounds strange, but you can act your way into feeling the right way. When you're busy doing the things you should, you'll find yourself wanting to do them because it makes you feel good about yourself. When you act like the person you want to be, pretty soon that is who you will be.

For the next week, make an extra effort to do the things you should do, be the person you want to be. At the end of the week, write down how you feel. Check back in a month.

CONTINUE TO THINK ABOUT THE THINGS THAT ARE GOOD AND WORTHY OF PRAISE. THINK ABOUT THE THINGS THAT ARE TRUE AND HONORABLE AND RIGHT AND PURE AND BEAUTIFUL AND RESPECTED.
—PHILIPPIANS 4:8

How you feel about yourself after the first week . . .

_____
_____
_____   NEVER GIVE UP.
_____   —EPHESIANS 6:18
_____

How you feel about yourself after a month . . .

_____
_____
_____
_____
_____

The Cure for a Wrong Attitude

Step 1

Say the right words,
Read the right books,
Listen to the right CDs,
Be with the right people,
Do the right things,
Pray the right prayer.

Step 2

Repeat Step 1 every day.

Should've, Could've, Would've

Do you ever find yourself thinking about what you should have done or could have done or would have done? It's a waste of time. The past is past, and no matter how much you think about it, you can't change it. The future, however, is up for grabs.

> I may not be able to change the world, but I can change the way I see the world.

Try this:

When you find yourself with a case of the "Should've, Could've, Would'ves," write down all those things that you wish you had done. When you've finished, shred the paper and throw it away. The past is past.

Write a prayer asking God to give you a right attitude in all things.

_____

_____

_____

_____

LIFE'S GREATEST
HAPPINESS
IS TO BE CONVINCED
THAT WE ARE LOVED.

—ViCTOR HUGO

5
That's What
I Like about You!

Good friends bonding.

The People Factor

The JOY of Leadership

You may have run across the JOY principle before—Jesus first, Others second, and Yourself last. This principle is great for everyone, but especially for those who want to lead. If you lead with JOY, you won't go wrong.

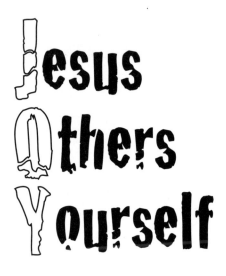

Jesus
Others
Yourself

What does JOY mean to you?

_____

_____

_____

_____

_____

_____

List some ways you can practice JOY with your friends . . .

_____

_____

_____

_____

your family . . .

_____

_____

_____

_____

someone you don't know very well . . .

_____

_____

_____

_____

even someone you don't particularly like . . .

_____

_____

_____

_____

My Influence

My life shall touch a dozen lives
before this day is done.
Leave countless marks of good or ill,
E'er sets the evening sun.

This, the wish I always wish,
The prayer I always pray:
Lord, may my life help other lives
It touches on the way.

—John C. Maxwell

Research has found that even the shyest person will touch the lives of more than ten thousand people. Sounds impossible, but it's true. Sometimes your contact with a person may last for years; other times it may be only a few seconds.

Make a list of all the people whose lives you touch—from family and friends to the store salesclerk to the guy who has a locker next to yours.

WYSIWYG

WYSIWYG—What You See Is What You Get. WYSIWYG not only applies to computers, it also applies to people. That is, what you think about people will largely decide how you treat them. And how you treat them can affect who they will be.

> **People tend to become what the most important people in their lives think they will become.**

Andrea was new at church. The first Sunday, she showed up in a leather skirt, wearing a chain that connected her earring to her nose ring. She wore army boots, and her hair was not a color found in nature. Everyone took one look and decided she was no good and didn't belong.

That first Sunday, Andrea tried to participate in the class discussions and talk to the other kids. She was obviously smart and knew a lot about the Bible, but no one could get past her appearance long enough to give her a chance. The second Sunday she was there, but said very little. Still no one talked *to* her—just *about* her. The third Sunday, she didn't come at all.

What would you do if someone very different walked into your class?

_____

_____

_____

_____

_____

_____

_____

_____

What would you do if you were the someone different? How would you want to be treated?

_____

_____

_____

_____

_____

_____

_____

_____

_____

Facts about Friends and Foes

Some things are true about virtually everyone—no matter how old they are, where they come from, or what they do.

FACT #1: Everyone wants to feel worthwhile and important.

Think of a person who makes you feel important and worthwhile.

How does he or she do that?

_____

_____

_____

_____

_____

How can you make others feel important? List some things—big or small—you can do every day to make others feel important.

_____

_____

_____

_____

FACT #2: Everyone needs encouragement.

Encouragement is oxygen to the soul. It brings out the best in people. Make it a daily goal to say something uplifting to others in the first sixty seconds of a conversation. That will set a positive tone for everything else and will make both of you feel better. You won't believe what a difference it will make.

What are some other ways you can encourage the people around you?

_____

_____

_____

_____

_____

What are some encouraging things you can say to your best friend?

_____

_____

_____

_____

_____

To your parents and family?

_____

_____

_____

To someone you don't really know?

_____

_____

My best friend is the one who brings out the best in me.
—Henry Ford

To someone you don't really like?

_____

_____

_____

Not only should you encourage others, but you should encourage yourself as well. Give yourself a pep talk every once in a while. Whenever you find yourself thinking something bad about yourself—*I'm too short, too tall; I'm too thin, too heavy; I hate my hair; Why do I have this huge zit on my face?*—say at least nine good things about yourself.

> It takes nine good comments to cancel out just one bad comment.

List at least 25 good things about yourself—more is even better!

1. _____
2. _____
3. _____
4. _____
5. _____
6. _____
7. _____
8. _____
9. _____
10. _____
11. _____
12. _____
13. _____
14. _____
15. _____
16. _____
17. _____
18. _____
19. _____
20. _____
21. _____
22. _____
23. _____
24. _____
25. _____

FACT #3: People "buy in" to you before they "buy in" to your leadership.

Until people believe you care about them, they will have no interest in following you or your ideas.

Think about the leaders in your life. How do they show that they care for you?

_____

_____

_____

_____

_____

FAILURE ONLY TRULY BECOMES FAILURE WHEN YOU DON'T LEARN FROM IT.

_____

_____

How can you show others that you care about them?

_____

_____

_____

_____

_____

_____

PEOPLE DO NOT CARE HOW MUCH YOU KNOW UNTIL THEY KNOW HOW MUCH YOU CARE.

FACT #4: Most people do not know how to succeed.

A lot of people think that success is just luck—like winning the lottery. But success is really the result of planning and hard work.

How do you think people succeed?

_____

_____

_____

_____

_____

_____

_____

A lot of people also think that success happens instantly. It doesn't. Success is a journey. It is achieving one thing and then using that as a steppingstone to achieve something else.

A lot of people think that success is learning how to never fail. But actually, the people who succeed are the ones who learn from their failures.

How have you learned from past failures and mistakes?

_____

_____

_____

_____

FACT #5: Most people want to learn, to explore, to be better people.

Little kids want to go to school. Three- and four-year-olds "play" school. They can't wait until they're old enough to actually go to school. And so off they go to kindergarten with brand-new backpacks, full of excitement. But after two or three years, some kids hate it. They make excuses not to go, complaining, "I don't feel good," or "My tummy hurts." What happened? Somehow their excitement was squashed. All the fun was gone.

As you choose things to do—and as you grow into a leader—remember to keep the excitement and fun in all that you do—and all that you ask others to do. After all, life's too short for you not to enjoy it. For example, if you need to earn some extra money, and you have a choice between baby-sitting—which you hate—or mowing the yard—which you like—then get out there and mow the yard!

Have you ever been really excited about doing something only to have your excitement squashed by someone else? Write your story here.

_____

_____

_____

_____

_____

Could anything have been done differently so that your excitement would not have been squashed? Or could you have reacted differently?

_____

_____

_____

_____

_____

Victor did it. He could hardly believe it, but he really did it. He made it to the final round of the skateboarding tournament, and he was pretty sure he had a shot at winning.

He was just checking his gear when one of the other contestants—a guy Victor had just put out of the tournament—came up to him.

"Ya know, even if you win, you won't really be the champion," the guy said.

"How's that?"

"The best guy out here—last year's champion—just hurt his knee on the last stunt and won't be able to compete in the finals. So, even if you win, you won't be the best 'cuz you didn't beat him."

As the guy walked away, Victor realized he didn't feel so excited or sure of himself anymore.

Why do you think that guy said what he did to Victor?

_____

_____

_____

_____

Do you think some people intentionally squash other people's excitement? Why?

_____

_____

_____

_____

Have you ever intentionally squashed someone's excitement? Why?

_____

_____

_____

_____

How to Take the Fun Out of Practically Anything

Of course, you don't really want to spoil anyone's fun and excitement, or make anyone feel worthless. Here are some ways to avoid that:

Don't put anyone down, especially in front of others. It's easy to make someone feel worthwhile and important, but it's even easier to make someone feel worthless and stupid. Remember, it takes nine positive comments to cancel out just one bad thing you say. Even something said as a joke can really hurt a person.

Write about a time when someone put you down.

_____

_____

_____

_____

How did you feel?

_____

_____

_____

_____

How long did it take you to get over what that person said about you?

_____

_____

_____

_____

A blow with a word
strikes deeper than a
blow with a sword.

—Robert Burton

Have you ever intentionally put someone else down?

_____

_____

_____

_____

What would you do differently if you had the chance?

_____

_____

_____

_____

Don't manipulate anyone. Trying to trick people into doing what you want only makes them distrust you. You'll get a lot farther by being honest with people, rather than being cunning and sneaky.

Write about a time when you were manipulated into doing something you didn't really want to do—perhaps by peer pressure.

_____

_____

_____

_____

_____

_____

How did you feel about the person who manipulated you?

_____

_____

_____

_____

_____

_____

Be a cheerleader. Instead of getting upset or jealous when someone does better than you, cheer her on. Don't feel threatened by the achievements of others; instead, try to take the team spirit approach that says, "The better you do, the better we all will do."

> A STRONGER
> PLAYER MAKES
> A STRONGER TEAM.

Hannah just perfected her routine on the uneven bars. You're still having trouble with yours, so the coach has decided you shouldn't compete in that event in the upcoming gymnastics meet. Hannah, on the other hand, has a good chance of winning a medal. As you're leaving, Hannah is right beside you.

What do you say to her?

_____

_____

_____

_____

_____

_____

Put people first. Take time to really get to know and care about people. They may surprise you with the things they can do.

Oh, great, Sam thought. *Twenty-six kids in this class, and I get stuck with Nathan the Nerd for a lab partner.*

For the next couple of weeks, Sam worked with Nathan in science lab, speaking to him as little as possible. Then, the worst happened—an out-of-class project. Nathan suggested a project on stars; he had a new telescope he wanted to try out.

That figures, thought Sam. *What self-respecting nerd wouldn't have a telescope!*

But when Sam arrived at Nathan's home and went up to his room, it wasn't what he expected. Posters of Pete Sampras, Andre Agassi, and other tennis greats covered one wall. On the other wall was a shelf full of tennis trophies.

"You play tennis?" Sam asked incredulously.

"Yeah, I love tennis."

"Me, too. But I'm not very good."

"I'd be glad to give you some tips some time," Nathan offered.

Has someone ever surprised you by being more than you expected him to be? How so?

_____

_____

_____

_____

Hey! Don't Do That!

There will be times when someone will do something that he or she shouldn't, and you will have to confront that person about it. Almost no one likes confrontation, but sometimes it has to be done. When you have to confront someone, keep these "ten commandments" in mind.

DO NOT BE INTERESTED ONLY IN YOUR OWN LIFE, BUT BE INTERESTED IN THE LIVES OF OTHERS.
—PHILIPPIANS 2:4

How do you feel about confronting people?

_____

_____

_____

_____

_____

Have you ever been confronted by someone? Did that person make you feel good or bad about yourself?

_____

_____

_____

_____

The Ten Commandments of Confrontation

1. Do it in private, not in front of others.

2. Don't put it off; do it as soon as possible.

3. Talk about only one issue at a time; don't overload the person with a long list of complaints.

4. Once you've made a point, don't keep repeating it.

5. Deal only with actions the person can change. For example, don't confront a person about her brother's behavior; she can't control what he does.

6. Don't be sarcastic.

7. Don't use words like "always" and "never."

8. Try to offer suggestions or ask questions instead of just saying, "You're wrong."

9. Don't apologize for confronting the person. He or she may not take you seriously if you do.

10. Don't forget the compliments. Try using the "sandwich" approach. That is, "sandwich" a negative comment between two compliments.

What's That You Say?

Listen, listen, listen. Stop talking and develop the art of really listening. Quit thinking of what you will say next, and begin to hear, not only what people say, but how they feel. Remember, what people really want is to be listened to, respected, and understood.

Are You a Good Listener?

- [ ] Do you allow the speaker to finish without interrupting?

- [ ] Do you listen "between the lines" for what the other person is feeling as well as saying?

- [ ] Do you repeat what the other person has just said to make sure you understood?

- [ ] Do you avoid getting mad if you disagree with what the other person is saying?

- [ ] Do you tune out distractions when listening?

- [ ] Do you make an effort to seem interested in what the other person is saying?

Jesus was—and is—the best listener ever. He listened to the woman at the well (John 4), He listened to the little children (Matthew 19), and He always listens to your prayers.

What can you do to become a better listener?

_____

_____

_____

_____

_____

_____

_____

Write a prayer asking God to help you treat people the way He would want you to.

_____

_____

_____

_____

_____

_____

_____

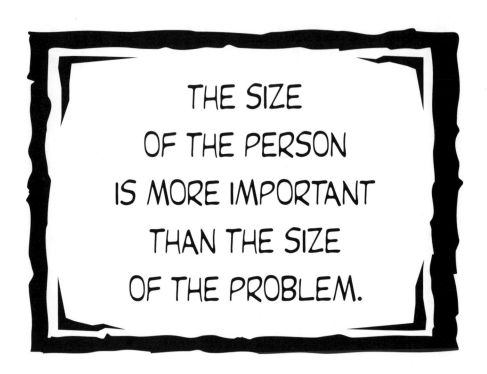

6
Bubble, Bubble, Toil & Trouble

Look on the bright side... some days are just more exciting.

What to Do When Problems Come Along

Problems, Problems Everywhere

Problems are *everywhere*, and *everybody* has them—the star jock, the head cheerleader, the straight-A student. Parents, teachers, friends—even you. So what do you do about them?

To solve problems, you need two things: a good attitude and a good plan.

Make a list of any problems—big or small—that you have in your life right now. As you go through this chapter, keep them in mind. You might just find a solution or two.

_____

_____

_____

_____

_____

_____

That Attitude Thing, Again

Yep, it's that attitude thing again. You can let problems ruin your life, or you can let problems bring meaning and change to your life. It's all in how you look at it.

Now, James had a good attitude! How do you think it is possible to be happy about your troubles?

_____

_____

_____

_____

_____

_____

MY BROTHERS, YOU WILL HAVE MANY KINDS OF TROUBLE. BUT WHEN THESE THINGS HAPPEN, YOU SHOULD BE VERY HAPPY. YOU KNOW THAT THESE THINGS ARE TESTING YOUR FAITH. AND THIS WILL GIVE YOU PATIENCE.

—JAMES 1:2-3

BUGViLLE, USA?

Consider the lowly boll weevil. Just a bug, right? Not even a cute bug. So why did the people of Enterprise, Alabama, build a statue in its honor?

In the South, when cotton was "king," the boll weevil crossed over from Mexico to the United States and destroyed the cotton plants. Farmers were forced to grow other crops, such as soybeans and peanuts. They learned to raise cattle, hogs, and chickens. As a result, many more farmers became prosperous than in the days when cotton was the only crop grown.

The people of Enterprise, Alabama, were so grateful for what had happened that in 1910 they built a statue in honor of the boll weevil. The inscription reads: "In profound appreciation of the boll weevil and what it has done to herald prosperity."

Now that *is* taking the right attitude!

Problems can be seen as problems, or they can be seen as opportunities. Look back at your list of problems. Write down any possible opportunities you see there.

_____

_____

_____

_____

_____

I WILL THANK YOU, LORD,
BECAUSE YOU ARE GOOD.
YOU HAVE SAVED ME
FROM ALL MY TROUBLES.
—PSALM 54:6-7

_____

_____

_____

_____

_____

_____

When you can't change your problem, change your perspective.

Problems Make You—*YOU*

Many outstanding people have overcome problems in their lives.

George Washington overcame the snows of Valley Forge. Abraham Lincoln overcame a lot of personal and economic disadvantages. Albert Einstein overcame having a learning disability (dyslexia) and being called slow and retarded.

Jesus overcame being born to a young girl in a smelly stable full of animals, having a king try to kill Him when He was still only a baby, having leaders plot against Him and eventually kill Him—only to rise from the grave to save us all.

Yes, even Jesus faced problems. He faced Satan and all his temptations. He put up with the Pharisees and their attempts to trap Him. He was poor, and He had no real home of His own. So, yes, Jesus knows what you're going through. And, yes, He's always there for you.

Think of some of the problems you've faced. How did they change you?

_____

_____

_____

_____

Are **YOU** the Problem?

There is a world of difference between a person who has a big problem and a person who makes a problem big.

Problems can stop you temporarily. But you are the only one who can do it permanently. You can't always choose what happens to you in life, but you can always choose your attitude

JESUS SAID,
"DON'T LET YOUR HEARTS
BE TROUBLED. TRUST IN
GOD. AND TRUST IN ME."
—**JOHN 14:1**

toward what happens. So, stop making excuses! Turn your problem into a steppingstone instead of a stumbling block.

There was a church choir that was raising money to attend a music competition and decided to have a car wash. But after a busy morning, rain began to pour midafternoon, and the customers stopped coming. Finally, one of the girls printed this poster:

Are you part of your problems?

_____

_____

_____

_____

_____

_____

_____

What will you do to be part of the answers?

_____

_____

_____

_____

_____

_____

_____

_____

_____

_____

_____

_____

_____

What Do You See?

"THE WiNDOW" BY G. W. TARGET
(adaptation)

Two men were in hospital beds in the same room. Both men were seriously ill and were not allowed to have television, radio, or books. Over time, they became friends. They talked about everything from family to jobs to vacations.

Neither man left his bed, but one was lucky enough to be next to the window. As part of his treatment he could sit up in bed for just an hour a day. At this time, he would describe the world outside to his roommate. As he spoke, he would bring the outside world inside to this friend, telling him all about the beautiful park he could see, with its lake, and the many interesting people he saw spending their time there. His friend began to live for these descriptions.

After a particularly fascinating report, the one man began to think it was not fair that his friend got to see everything while he could see nothing. He was ashamed of his thoughts, but he had quite a bit of time to think and he couldn't get this out of his mind. After a while, his thoughts began to have an effect on his health and he became even more ill—and bitter.

One evening his friend, who sometimes had a hard time breathing, awoke with a fit of coughing and choking and was unable to push the button for the nurse to come and help him. The angry, sour man lay there looking at the ceiling, listening to this struggle for life next to him, and doing nothing.

The next morning the day nurse came in to find the man by the window dead.

The man who was so eager to see out that window asked if he could be moved, and it was quickly done. As soon as the room was empty, the man struggled up on his elbow to look out the window and fill his spirit with the sights of the outside world.

It was then he discovered the window faced a blank wall.

So what do **YOU** see when you look out your window?

_____

_____

_____

_____

_____

Think back to the problems you listed at the beginning of this chapter. How could a change in attitude help you to see these problems differently?

_____

_____

_____

_____

_____

Positive thinking does not always change the problem, but it will always change you.

Planning the Good Plan

Life is not problem-free, so it's important to develop a good plan for tackling life's little—and not-so-little—problems. Here are a few tips.

1. Find out the real problem.

Too many times we attack the symptoms of the problem, not the real problem (or problems). List all the possible causes of the problem by asking what caused the problem and how it can be avoided in the future.

> Anthony is getting Cs and Ds in history. He's not happy about it, his teacher isn't happy, and his parents definitely aren't happy. They all know Anthony can do better, but how?
>
> Actually, the not-so-great grades in history are only a symptom. What's the real problem? Anthony writes down everything he can think of that affects his history grade—things that happen in class, things that happen while he's studying, things that might keep him from studying. He then asks his parents and teachers what they think might be causing his poor grades. Together, they come up with this list:
>
> ⛛ Since Anthony doesn't particularly like history, he often waits to read his homework until right before he goes to bed. Sometimes he reads in bed and falls asleep in the middle of his homework.

- And because history bores Anthony, he often listens to music or the television while he reads.

- Anthony doesn't always turn in his homework.

- And last, there is a girl in history class whom Anthony really likes, and he often spends more time passing notes to her than listening to the teacher.

Take one of the problems you wrote down on page 122. Is it a symptom or a problem? Brainstorm about what might be causing your problem. Write your thoughts here.

2. Decide where to start.

Now that you have a list of the real problems, you can begin trying to solve them. But it's best not to tackle them all at once. First, decide which problem is the most important—or the biggest—and start there.

Looking over his list, Anthony decides the real problem is his poor study habits. He decides to start there.

Where will you start on your problem?

3. Figure out how to fix the problem.

Now you know which problem to start with, but what do you do about it? Time for some more brainstorming. Write down as many possible solutions to your problem as you can. The more, the better. Rarely is there only one way to solve a problem. It's always good to have a backup solution, in case the first one doesn't work. And don't forget to ask around—maybe others have had a similar problem or have ideas for how to help with yours.

Anthony—with the help of his teachers and parents—came up with this list of possible solutions for his poor study habits.

- ☐ Study earlier in the day.

- ☐ Study where it is quiet.

- ☐ Take breaks to avoid getting bored.

- ☐ Do all homework and assignments on time.

- ☐ Talk to the girl he likes before and after class instead of passing notes in class.

List all the possible solutions you can think of to your problem.

4. Go with the best.

Now that you have all these possible solutions, it's time to pick the best one. Ask yourself:

☐ Which one has the greatest chance of success?

☐ Which one is in my best interests?

☐ Which one has timing on its side?

Look over your list of possible solutions. Which one do you think will work best for your problems?

_____

_____

_____

_____

_____

_____

_____

_____

_____

_____

Now Go Do It!

Write a prayer asking God to help in times of trouble.

WHEN YOU'RE
THROUGH CHANGING,
YOU'RE THROUGH.

7
Change!?!

I Don't Need No Change! Or Do I?

Everything Changes

Yep. It's a fact. Change happens. Big changes, little changes; good changes, bad changes. And sooner or later, it will happen to you.

The only thing that never changes is the fact that everything changes.

What are some changes that have happened to you in the last week? Month? Year?

_____

_____

_____

_____

_____

_____

_____

_____

How did you feel about the possibility of the changes before they happened?

_____

_____

_____

_____

_____

How about after?

_____

_____

_____

_____

_____

_____

_____

Did they turn out to be good changes or bad changes?

_____

_____

_____

_____

_____

Ready or Not, Here Comes . . .
CHANGE!

_____   _____
your writing hand   *your other hand*

Directions:

1. Write the word attitude *on the left line with your "writing" hand.*

2. Write the word attitude *on the right line with your other hand.*

When you look at the word attitude *written by the hand you do not usually write with, you see a picture of the kind of attitude we often have when we are faced with change. A little shaky, and things don't go quite the way we want them to go.*

There is nothing harder than change. And at some point, everyone tries to avoid change—even good change.

Write about a time when you tried to avoid change. Did it work?

_____

_____

_____

_____

Have you ever wanted to make a change that other people tried to avoid (like a change to a later curfew that your parents didn't go for)? What did you do?

_____

_____

_____

_____

_____

_____

The Top Ten Reasons People Avoid Change

1. It wasn't my idea!

It's pretty hard to be open to a change that is forced upon you—like having to give up your favorite skateboarding spot because they're building a parking garage on it, or having to move across town to be closer to your dad's work.

Write about a change that wasn't your idea. Were you excited or reluctant about the change?

_____

_____

_____

_____

2. It messes up my way of doing things.

We all have habits, ways we prefer to do things. Change sometimes messes those up. It forces us to think differently and to act outside our comfort zones.

Behind Kevin's house, there's a huge field—perfect for dirt biking with his friends, which they do two or three times a week. One day, a sign goes up: Coming Soon—Woodland Acres Subdivision. Then, just a few days later, bulldozers are tearing up the field, and trucks are hauling in construction supplies. No more dirt biking here. Kevin definitely didn't like this change!

How has a change messed up your way of doing things?

_____

_____

_____

_____

_____

_____

First we form habits, but then our habits form us.

3. But what will happen?

Change means traveling in uncharted waters, and this causes our fears and insecurities to appear.

For the last two years, Amy has played on her school's softball team—and has done pretty well. Her coach thinks she should play with a traveling softball team over the summer. Amy's not sure. The level of competition is a lot higher on these teams, plus she wouldn't know anyone else on the team. Amy worries that she might not be good enough.

When faced with a change, what kinds of things do you worry about?

_____

_____

_____

_____

_____

_____

4. Why do I have to change?

It's especially hard to accept a change when you don't understand why things need to change.

Lance has just started at Lincoln High—it's where his older brother went, too, and he's heard lots of stories about the fun times his brother has had. But yesterday, he read in the newspaper that the school board has decided to turn Lincoln High into a middle school next year. Lincoln High's students will be divided between two different schools in the county. Lance isn't even sure if he'll end up at the same school as his friends. The paper listed lots of statistics and numbers, but it still didn't make sense to Lance.

Have you ever been faced with a change you didn't understand? How did it make you feel?

_____

_____

_____

_____

_____

_____

5. What if I mess it up?

Everyone makes mistakes. But look at it this way: Failure is just the opportunity to begin again more intelligently.

> ### The greatest mistake a person can make is to be afraid of making one.
> —Elbert Hubbard

Do you worry about making mistakes in new situations?

_____

_____

_____

_____

_____

_____

It is tragic
when success
goes to your head;
but it is even more tragic
when failure
goes to your head.

6. I like it the way it is!

It's always more comfortable to stay with the known than to go with the unknown—even if the unknown may end up being more comfortable and better. Take graduating from high school. It's fun and exciting, but it's also challenging. On the other hand, who wants to stay a high school student forever?

"I've always done it this way, and it works just fine for me."

Have you ever said something like this?

_____

_____

_____

_____

_____

7. I like my idea better.

It's easy to think your idea is the best. After all, you thought of it, right?

Michaela has just been put in charge of planning the entertainment for an upcoming lock-in for her church's youth group. She comes up with the idea of having a costume party. Everyone thinks this is a good idea until Leann suggests having a murder mystery party. Now everyone is ignoring Michaela's idea, and she is less than happy about it.

Write about a time when one of your ideas was shot down in favor of someone else's. Were you excited about the other idea?

_____

_____

_____

_____

_____

8. But what about me?

Whenever change is coming, it's only natural to ask, "What about me? How will this affect me?" Fact is that sometimes you will lose, sometimes it won't affect you at all, and sometimes you will come out ahead.

Think about a time when you thought a change would be bad, but instead it had a good effect on your life. Write about that change.

_____

_____

_____

_____

9. It's too hard; it's not worth it.

People won't change unless they see that the advantages of changing outweigh the disadvantages of keeping things the way they are.

Karen has had the same softball glove for years. It fits her hand perfectly. The problem is that it fell out of her equipment bag and was lost outside for over a week. It's still usable, but it's not in very good shape. Karen's dad has offered to buy her a new one, but it would take weeks to break in a new glove. She isn't sure what she wants to do.

Have you ever wondered if it was worth it to make a change?

_____

_____

_____

_____

_____

10. It'll never work.

This is the person who never thinks anything new will work, especially if it wasn't his or her idea!

A great new wrestling move? "It'll never work." A chance for your Sunday school class to tackle a really big project—helping build a house for the poor? "It'll never work." No matter what the change, this person declares, "It'll never work."

Do you know someone like this? What do you think about this kind of attitude?

_____

_____

_____

**DON'T LOOK—YOU MIGHT SEE.
DON'T LISTEN—YOU MIGHT HEAR.
DON'T THINK—YOU MIGHT LEARN.
DON'T MAKE A DECISION—YOU MIGHT BE WRONG.
DON'T WALK—YOU MIGHT STUMBLE.
DON'T RUN—YOU MIGHT FALL.
DON'T LIVE—YOU MIGHT DIE.
DON'T CHANGE—YOU MIGHT GROW.**

What to Do When Change Gets in Your Face

When a big change is headed your way, try this. Make a list of all the advantages and disadvantages of the change. Then make another list telling all the ways you feel about the change. This will help you see exactly how the change will affect you and whether or not the change makes sense. You may just find yourself saying, "I could go for this change." And even if you don't, you'll know exactly how you feel and why, which will help you when talking to others about the change—or when you're trying to talk others out of making the change.

Think of a change that is coming your way.

List the advantages:

_____

_____

_____

_____

_____

_____

_____

List the disadvantages:

_____

_____

_____

_____

_____

_____

_____

List your feelings about the change.

Good feelings

_____

_____

_____

_____

_____

_____

_____

Bad feelings

_____

_____

_____

_____

_____

_____

_____

How will the change affect you?

Good ways	Bad ways
_____	_____
_____	_____
_____	_____
_____	_____
_____	_____
_____	_____
_____	_____
_____	_____
_____	_____

Now that you've looked at the advantages and disadvantages, does the change seem like a good idea or a bad one?

_____

_____

_____

_____

_____

_____

Serenity Prayer

God grant me the
SERENITY
to accept the things
I cannot change,
COURAGE
to change the things I can, and
WISDOM
to know the
difference.

—Reinhold Niebuhr

I Wanna Try . . .

Sometimes you will be the one who wants to change something. Maybe you want to start working as a baby-sitter for your neighbors, or play basketball on your school team instead of your church team, or even just cut your hair a different way. It's still a good idea to stop and ask yourself a few questions.

Ready for Change?

1. Will this change be good for me?
2. Is this change in line with my goals for myself and my future?
3. Do I know all the details of this change?
4. Can I do a test run before I make a permanent change?
5. If the change doesn't work, can I go back to the way things were before?
6. Is this a good time to try the change?

Is there a change that you've been considering? Apply the questions above to it. Now, does the change still seem like a good idea?

_____

_____

_____

_____

_____

How Can I Change Someone Else?

Sometimes you really want to change another person—or to help them change. That's okay—as long as you are doing it to help them and not just for yourself. Maybe you want to help that shy girl in your algebra class to be more outgoing, or maybe you'd like to change the way your parents treat you so that they act like you're not just a kid. But how do you go about changing someone else, especially if they don't want to change?

It all starts with you. As a leader, you've got to be willing to make changes in yourself, before people will trust you enough to make changes in them. The more you change, the more you will help others to change. After all, great leaders not only say what should be done, they do it!

Is there something that you would like to change about someone? What is it and why?

_____

_____

_____

_____

_____

_____

YOU'VE GOT TO LOVE 'EM BEFORE YOU CAN LEAD 'EM.

How do you think this person will react to the change?

_____

_____

_____

_____

_____

_____

_____

_____

_____

What can you do to encourage this person to change?

_____

_____

_____

_____

_____

_____

_____

_____

_____

_____

_____

The Master Changer

Jesus was—and is—a master at getting people to change. When He called Peter and Andrew to be His disciples, He asked them to leave their fishing and follow Him—completely changing their lives (Matthew 4:18–20). Jesus told His followers to change the way they treated people when He told them to love their enemies as well as their neighbors (Matthew 5:43–48). He told people not to judge others (Matthew 7:1–2), not to worry (Matthew 6:25–32), and to seek God first (Matthew 6:33).

> YOU CAN BE SURE THAT I WILL BE WITH YOU ALWAYS.
> —MATTHEW 28:20

The New Testament is filled with Jesus' challenges to change. And it's not easy. Yet millions of people do it. Why? Because Jesus has already proved His love, and because He is always right there with His followers, showing them the way.

How has Jesus changed you?

_____

_____

_____

_____

_____

_____

Who, Me? Change?

Everyone has something he or she would like to change about themselves. Maybe you'd like to be more outgoing, try playing the saxophone instead of the clarinet, or learn to be a better Bible student.

Write down some things you would like to change about yourself.

_____

_____

_____

List some people who can help you make these changes.

_____

_____

_____

Write a prayer asking for God's guidance when you face change.

_____

_____

_____

_____

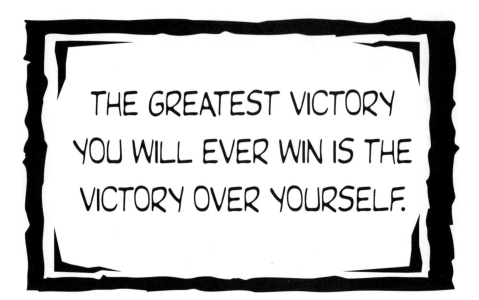

THE GREATEST VICTORY
YOU WILL EVER WIN IS THE
VICTORY OVER YOURSELF.

8
Get a Grip!

Oh, great. Time to get up and conquer that first-period math test!

I wonder if Einstein got started this way?

© BOBBY GOMBERT 2001

Taking Control of Life

Getting a Grip on Self-Control

The Greek word for *self-control* comes from a root word meaning "to grip" or "take hold of." This word describes people who are willing to get a grip on their lives and take responsibility for who they are and what they do.

The number one responsibility of a leader—of anyone, really—is to take responsibility for his or her own self-discipline and self-control. After all, if you can't lead yourself, you certainly can't lead others.

Discipline begins by doing things that you know you should do, but that you don't really want to do. This can take years of practice.

What are some areas of your life that need a little more self-discipline? These could be anything, such as practicing your sports or music, spending daily time with God, studying more, and avoiding gossip.

GOD . . . GAVE US A SPIRIT OF POWER AND LOVE AND SELF-CONTROL.
—2 TIMOTHY 1:7

BUT THE SPIRIT GIVES LOVE, JOY, PEACE, PATIENCE, KINDNESS, GOODNESS, FAITHFULNESS, GENTLENESS, SELF-CONTROL.

— GALATIANS 5:22-23

SO PREPARE YOUR MINDS FOR SERVICE AND HAVE SELF-CONTROL.

—1 PETER 1:13

How to Develop Self-Discipline: Start with Yourself

A reporter once asked the great evangelist D. L. Moody which people gave him the most trouble. He immediately answered, "I've had more trouble with D. L. Moody than any man alive."

Do you ever get yourself into trouble? How?

_____

_____

_____

_____

_____

_____

What have you learned from those times?

_____

_____

_____

_____

_____

The foolish want to conquer the world; the wise want to conquer themselves. If you could kick the person responsible for most of your troubles, you wouldn't be able to sit down for weeks.

Start Early

Perhaps the most valuable thing you can learn is the ability to make yourself do the thing you have to do, when you ought to do it, whether you like it or not. It is the first lesson that *ought* to be learned, but it's probably the last one that *is* learned.

Do the little things
before they get to be big things.
It's not hard to wash out a dirty dish.
But if you wait a couple of weeks
until you need it again,
it can get really gross!

What are some little things that you've let become big things?

_____

_____

_____

_____

_____

_____

_____

What could you have done differently to avoid this?

_____

_____

_____

_____

_____

_____

_____

_____

_____

_____

_____

Start Small

If you will begin developing self-discipline in a small way today, you will be self-disciplined in a big way tomorrow.

THiNK BiG,

BUT START SMALL.

A Small Plan That Will Make a Big Difference

1. List five areas in your life that lack discipline.

A. _____

B. _____

C. _____

D. _____

E. _____

2. Place them in the order you want to work on them.

A. _____

B. _____

C. _____

D. _____

E. _____

3. Take them on, one at a time. Work on one area for sixty days before going on to the next. This will keep you from becoming overwhelmed.

> ### Having it all doesn't mean having it all at once.

Why do you think it's important to tackle just one area at a time?

_____

_____

_____

_____

Which will you work on first?

_____

_____

_____

_____

_____

4. Ask a person who models the trait you would like to have to hold you accountable for it.

For example, if you really admire the way Gabrielle spends daily prayer time with God, ask her if she would mind helping you to learn to do the same. Often, just having someone who will check on your progress, who will hold you accountable, will give you the extra incentive to keep on the right path. Without someone holding you accountable, it's easy to just forget about it and go back to the old way.

Who can you ask to help you with the first area you want to work on? What is it about this person that will make him or her good at holding you accountable?

_____

_____

_____

_____

_____

5. **Spend fifteen minutes each morning focusing on the area of your life that you are working on.** A great way to do this is to spend this time with God, asking for His help.

Write a prayer to God asking for His help for today.

_____

_____

_____

_____

_____

6. **Keep a journal.** Take five minutes before you go to bed to jot down your progress for the day. If you get discouraged, go back to those first days and see just how far you've come. Your journal could look something like this:

My goal is

_____

_____

_____

_____

_____

_____

Date	How I Did Today
_____	_____
_____	_____
_____	_____
_____	_____
_____	_____
_____	_____
_____	_____
_____	_____
_____	_____
_____	_____

7. **Celebrate your successes!** Treat yourself (and the friend who is helping you to be accountable) to a special reward.

How will you celebrate your successes?

_____

_____

_____

_____

_____

What you are going to be tomorrow, you are becoming today.

Start Now

Don't wait until tomorrow or until you feel like it. Stop making excuses and start now.

What will you do today to work on your self-discipline?

_____

_____

_____

_____

_____

_____

_____

Before you can become a "star," you have to start.

Get Organized

Organize is a popular word these days. You hear it everywhere. But what it really boils down to is making the most of your time and energy. Here are some tips:

☐ Do the most important things first and the least important things last.

☐ Put important events and deadlines on a calendar, and share it with your family, so they can help keep you on track.

☐ Don't wait until the last minute; allow time for the unexpected.

☐ Tackle just one project at a time, so that you don't get overwhelmed.

☐ Set up your own workspace with everything you need close by—pencils, paper, dictionary—maybe even a snack or two.

- Find out what works for you. When do you do your best studying? When is the best time for you to spend with friends?
- Have a plan for downtime. E-mail a friend, call someone, read a book. Use car rides as a time to talk to your parents.
- Focus on getting results, not just staying busy. Spend your time doing the important.
- Be responsible for who you are, and what you do.

What will you do to be better organized?

_____

_____

_____

I am only one,
But still I am one.
I cannot do everything,
But still I can do something.
And because I cannot
do everything
I will not refuse to do the
something that I can do.

—Edward Everett Hale

Pay Now, Play Later

There are two ways to go. You can pay now and play later, or you can play now and pay later. Either way there will be consequences for your actions; the only question is whether the consequences will be good or bad. It's up to you.

Write about a time when you played first and then had to pay later. How did it work out?

_____

_____

_____

_____

_____

_____

Would you do it differently next time? How?

_____

_____

_____

_____

_____

_____

_____

Who's Driving, Anyway?

Are you character-driven or emotion-driven? That is, do you do what needs to be done when it needs to be done (character-driven)? Or do you wait until you *feel* like doing what needs to be done (emotion-driven)? It is not doing the things we *like* to do, but doing the things we *need* to do that makes us a successful person and a good leader.

Read over these characteristics of character-driven people and emotion-driven people.

Character-Driven People

- [ ] Do right, then feel good
- [ ] Do what they need to do
- [ ] Make decisions based on their goals
- [ ] Control their attitude
- [ ] Take the first step
- [ ] Ask: "What can I do for you?"
- [ ] Keep going when problems come up
- [ ] Are leaders

Emotion-Driven People

- [ ] Feel good, then do right
- [ ] Do what they feel like doing
- [ ] Make decisions based on what everyone else is doing
- [ ] Are controlled by their attitude
- [ ] Wait for someone else to take the first step
- [ ] Ask: "What can you do for me?"
- [ ] Are stopped by problems
- [ ] Are followers

Are you character-driven or emotion-driven?

_____

_____

_____

What can you do to become more character-driven?

_____

_____

_____

_____

_____

_____

Write a prayer asking God to mold you into the person He wants you to be.

_____

_____

_____

_____

_____

Well, you've come to the end of this journal. We've talked a lot about leadership and your journey. Now it's time for you to go forward and apply what you've learned about leadership to your life. It's time to start leading from the lockers.

The End?

Nope...

just the beginning ...
so, Get out there, and start

Leading from the lockers!